ANCIENT TREASURE MAZES

DAVE PHILLIPS

DOVER PUBLICATIONS, INC.
Mineola, New York

Note

Every corner of the world is full of undiscovered treasure. But where there is adventure, discovery, and potential wealth, there are also challenges, menaces, and obstacles to overcome. Archaeologists may search for and find long-hidden gold and jewels, yet there are many discoveries worth more than their weight in conventional treasure. In fact, the greatest treasures reveal new truths about our history and our very nature.

Your quest is to brave the many dangers that lurk along the twisting paths of the thirty-six mazes in this unique book. As you set off, strive to make the right choices and take the turns that lead to fabulous treasure, but beware—a hastily chosen path often leads to disaster and doom. A Solutions section begins on page 37, but don't peek until you've tried your hardest. Good luck to you!

Copyright

Copyright © 2009 by Dave Phillips
All rights reserved.

Bibliographical Note

Ancient Treasure Mazes is a new work, first published by Dover Publications, Inc., in 2009.

International Standard Book Number
ISBN-13: 978-0-486-46773-3
ISBN-10: 0-486-46773-2

Manufactured in the United States of America
Dover Publications, Inc., 31 East 2nd Street, Mineola, N.Y. 11501

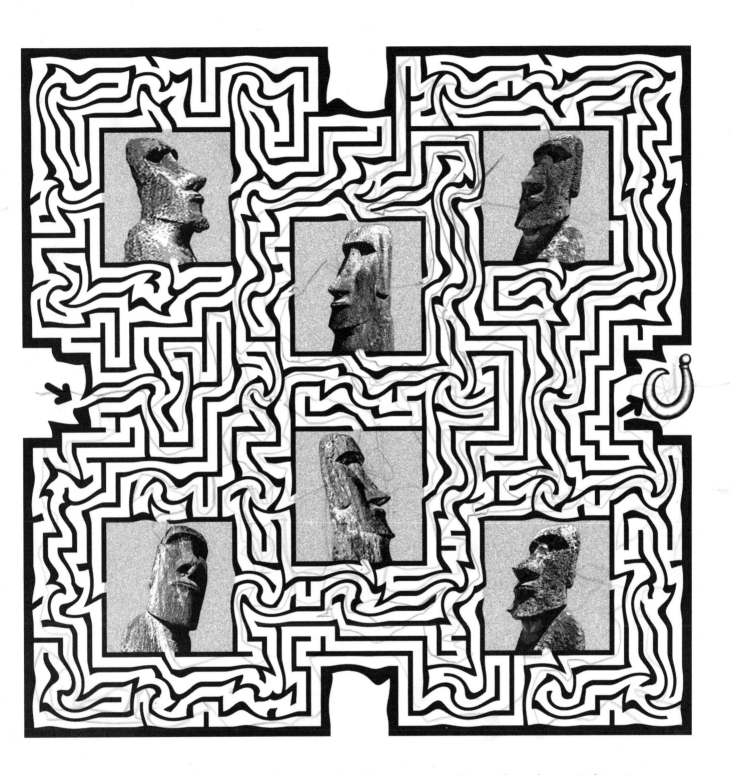

The giant stone statues on Easter Island were carved by a long-lost civilization. Many visitors walk paths where the massive figures still stand in silent vigil, but you seek a small treasure lost since the time the statues were set in place: a simple stone hook used by the mysterious builders.

Millennia of shifting desert sands can bury all traces of ancient human habitation. But the wayward winds may also reveal secret, long-hidden places. Your mission is to find a newly exposed ancient tomb. Take care not to lose yourself to the timeless desert.

The Great Wall of China stretches 4,000 miles long, and many years into the past. Hidden treasures await discovery along its meandering course through the mountains, but beware the wolves prowling in the night.

There are many ancient sites of mysterious standing stones throughout Europe. These prehistoric sites contain nearby barrows where powerful chiefs were buried, along with their prized possessions. However, access to these sites is well protected by law, allowing entry only to the most accomplished archaeologists. But the hidden meaning of sites such as Stonehenge continues to lure the curious.

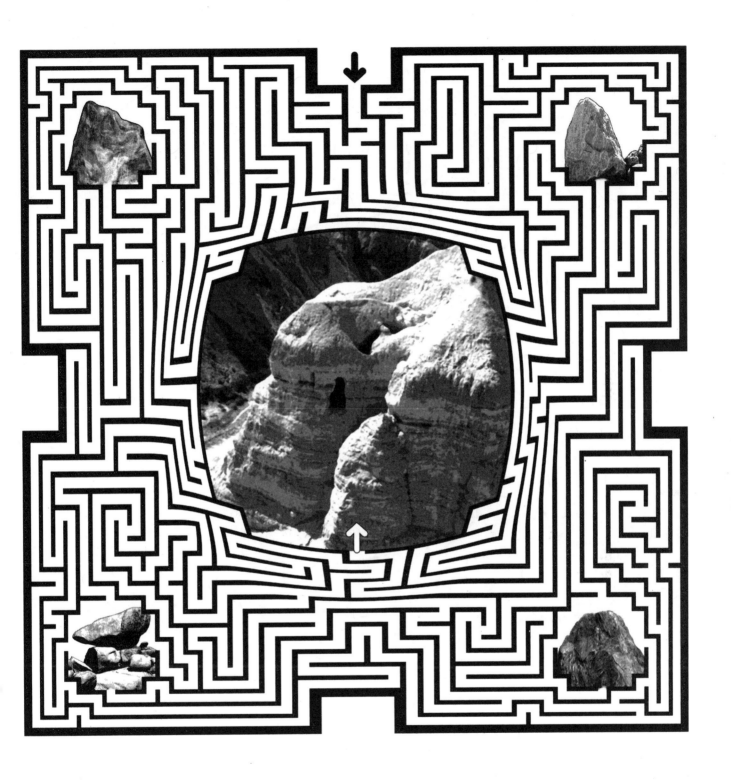

Natural caves perch high on the hills near the Dead Sea. Ancient scrolls—written treasures of a lost people—have been discovered within them. These hiding places were chosen well, although a single slip by the seeker may mean a fatal fall to the jagged rocks below.

Before the arrival of Europeans in the Americas, native peoples built cliff-cities at Mesa Verde in Colorado. These amazing, long-deserted communities were sheltered from the elements by overhanging cliffs. Though artifacts may be found there, shelter from a violent storm is also of great value.

Many ancient temples and palaces lie in ruins, damaged by earthquakes. A few columns stand in testimony to the wonders of the architecture they once supported. It is best not to explore such crumbling ruins for treasure during one of these earthquakes, however: it is far better to escape with your life.

The Sphinx of ancient Egypt has lain buried at different times during its history, inviting treasure hunters to seek hidden chambers filled with untold riches. Your task is to reach the Sphinx, while escaping the clutches of desert bandits.

One of the greatest treasures ever found is a broken tablet called the Rosetta Stone; scholars used it to decipher Egyptian hieroglyphics. It was discovered during the military campaign of Napoleon. Carefully make your way to the Rosetta Stone, but stay clear of the battle.

Many treasures yet lie at the bottom of the sea. Whether sunk by storm or by war, ancient ships bearing plundered treasure await discovery by those who possess the technology, luck, and daring to reach them. Are you one of them?

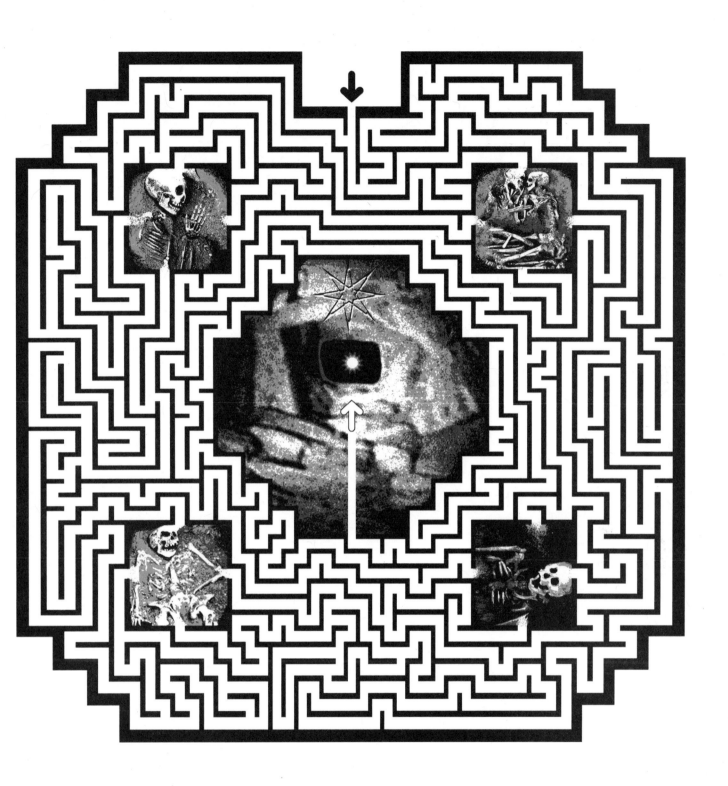

There exist labyrinthian tunnels under the earth, both natural and man-made. If the light fails, panic and a slow death in the dark may claim foolhardy adventurers. Find the way out to the light, since the greatest treasure of all may be your life.

In desolate, rocky terrain, ancient temples and sanctuaries were built into the living rock. Such places may contain hidden treasures for those who can find their way amidst a maze of treacherous paths. Perhaps you will succeed as well.

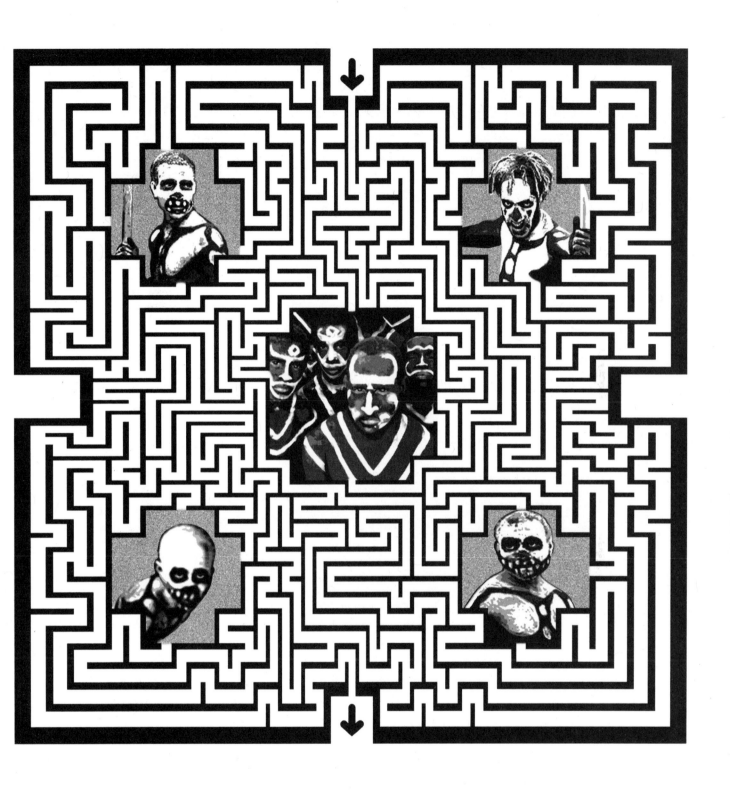

Lost cities and fallen civilizations contain valuable artifacts, but they often are guarded by those who distrust the intrusions of treasure seekers who may defile the sacred places of their ancestors. Find a path to avoid them.

Newer civilizations may build on top of the old, frequently burying considerable treasure beneath contemporary junk. An ancient Celtic ring lies beneath a pile of modern debris. Can you sift through the trash to find the treasure?

A valuable Roman coin was carelessly dropped centuries ago into a tangle of rusting chains. Only a careful excavation of piles of worthless metal will produce the reward of this precious bounty.

When an adventurous archaeologist delves deeply along forbidden paths to find a golden prize, booby traps should be expected. Thinly covered pits lined with spikes lie in wait through the centuries for a victim.

One of the oldest coins in the world—displaying a lion's head on one side—was handstruck 2,700 years ago. To claim it, you must invade a colony of bats. Perhaps the bats' ancestors caused the original owner to drop it in careless haste . . .

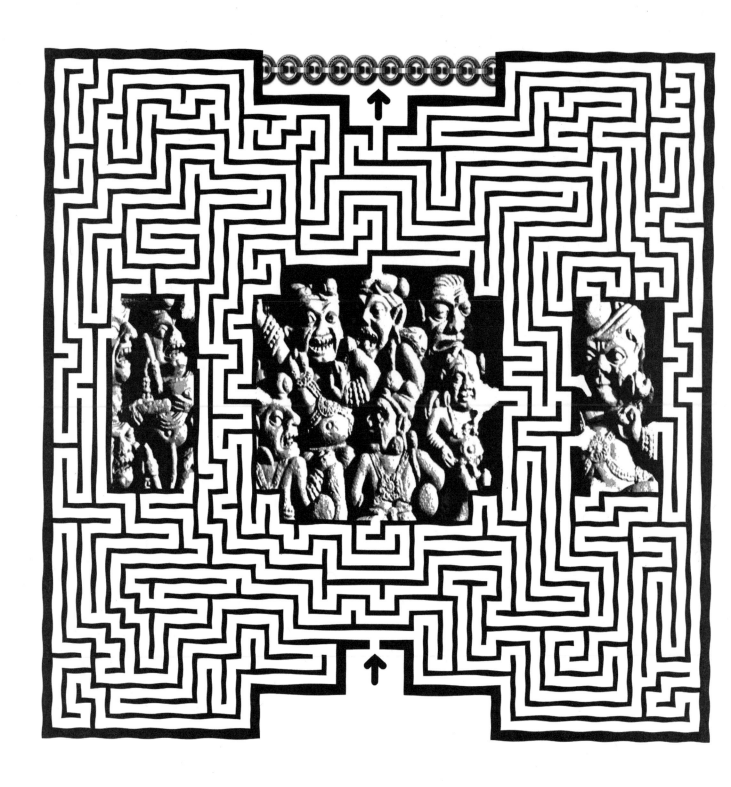

Fear of curses, ghosts, and evil spirits may still have power over the minds of the superstitious. Even the bravest among us may be daunted by the unseen and imagined. Find your way past frightful, yet (presumably) powerless, carvings to find a precious link chain.

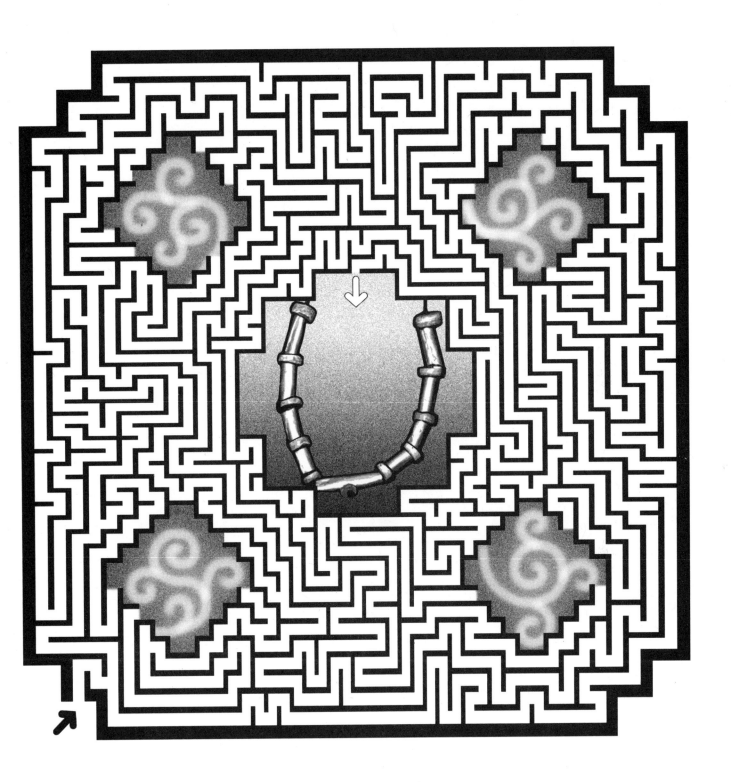

The unseen may often be a danger. Inside a chamber, locked away for many a century, is the oldest golden necklace discovered in South America. The air trapped in the chamber has turned poisonous over the centuries. Beware—the inexperienced may rush in too soon, only to find their doom.

An artifact of great value—an ancient helmet of a Greek hero—awaits discovery by the one who can decipher the clues carved into a circular stone. The clues are designed to lead the worthy to a lost tomb, leaving others to wander helplessly in circles.

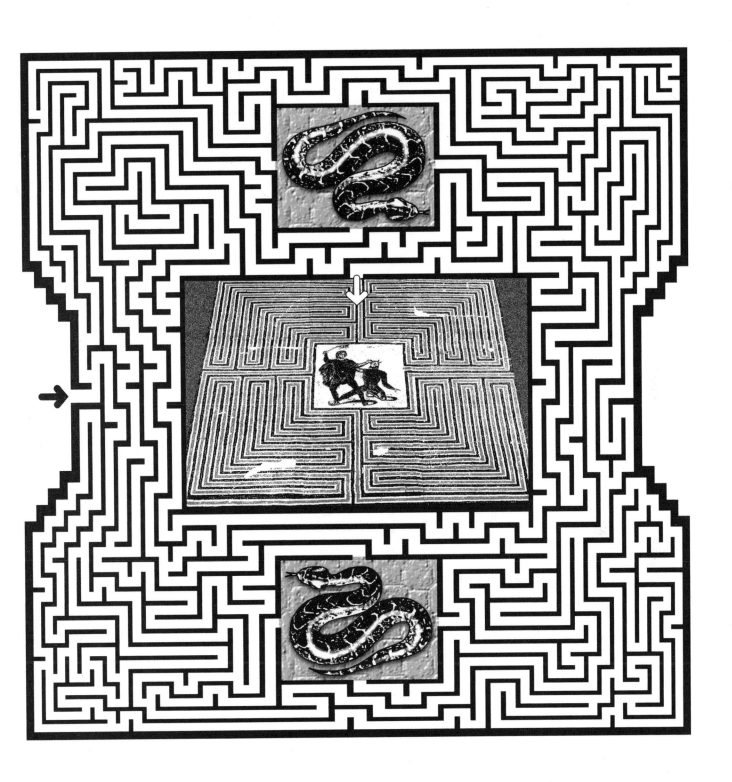

A Roman tile design depicts the fabled maze of the Minotaur, a half-man, half-bull creature trapped by King Minos. This treasure posesses great historic value, but a warning to those in pursuit: poisonous adders also slither over the ancient tiles.

Hidden in chambers, buried for the ages, are ancient Egyptian tombs and temples containing priceless, unread hieroglyphics. Make your way with great care, as certain mummies are said to possess powers beyond the grave.

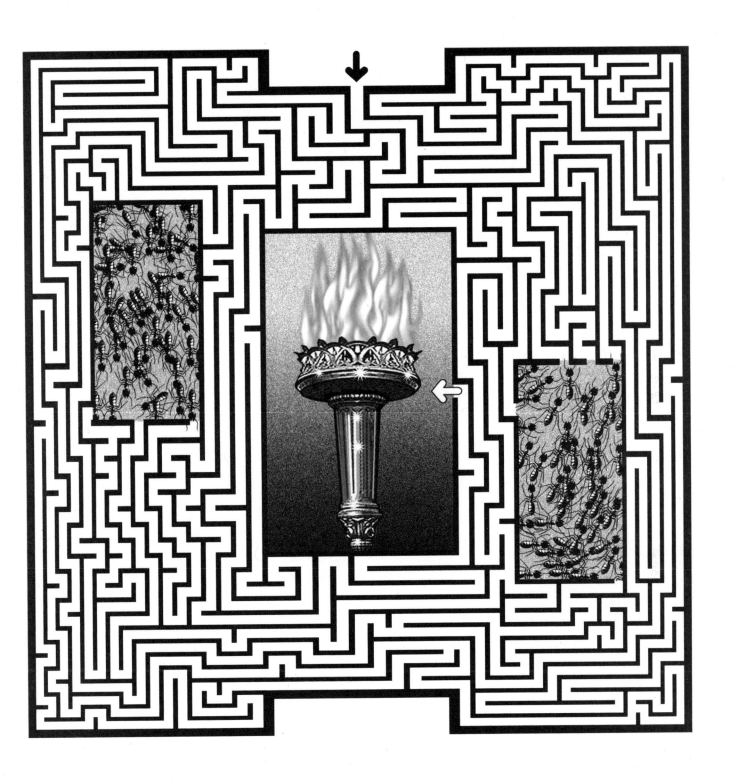

The prize, a golden torch, once was used in an ancient ceremony. It must be claimed not only as a treasure but also as a weapon whose flame will ward off an army of soldier ants that will devour anything in their path—including you.

Fire is an ever-present danger to centuries-old, tinder-dry materials such as parchment, wood, and cloth. A spark may ignite a fire that will quickly consume irreplaceable treasures. Do your best to reach the precious roll of ancient parchment before the hungry fire consumes it.

Lost cities, claimed by the jungle, may yet give up their secrets to those who dare to make a path through the tangled maze of vines and brush. Exhaustion and many other hazards will claim your life if you stray too far into the jungle in pursuit of the majestic tablet.

An ancient army of life-sized clay soldiers was discovered several decades ago in China. This great treasure contains thousands of likenesses, no two the same. Buried since the time of the first emperor, these amazing artifacts are threatened by a potential collapse of the surrounding walls and ceilings. Archaeologists and fortune-seekers alike should fear for their safety as well.

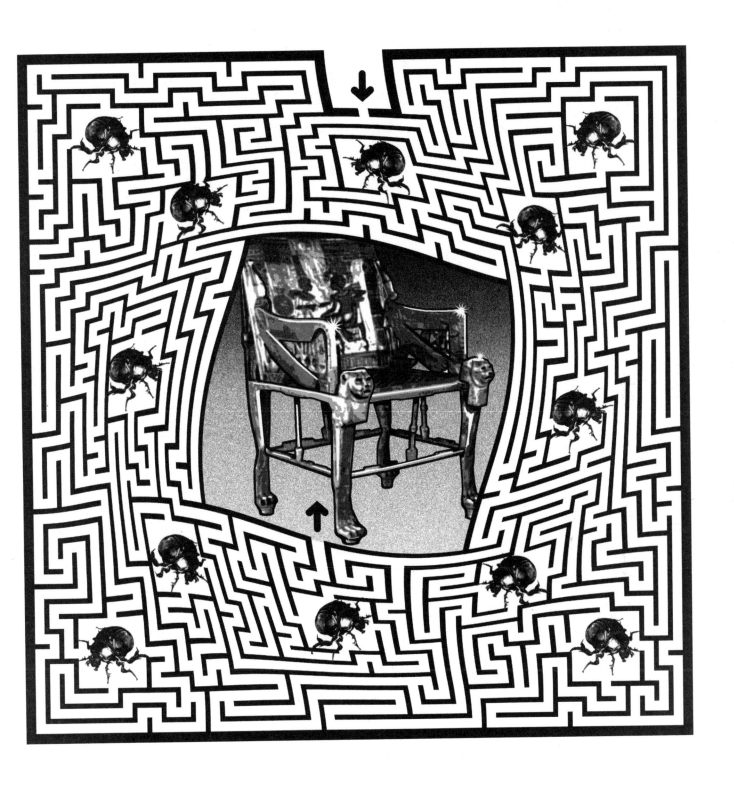

This majestic golden throne served as the seat of kings and queens, as well as being a symbol of authority and power. To claim this treasure, however, you must invade a domain long inhabited by creatures best not disturbed.

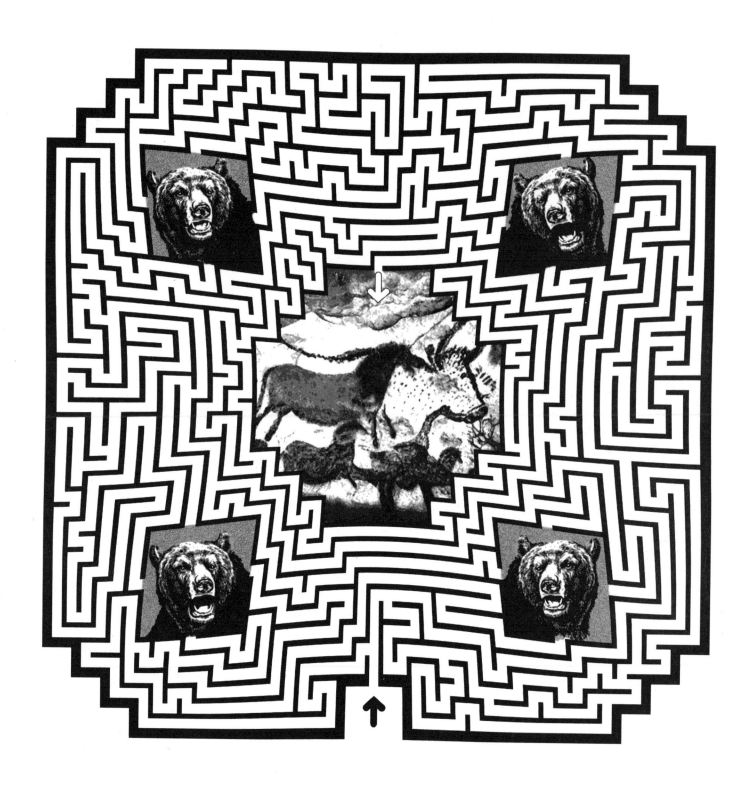

Great paintings have an honored place among the treasures of the world. The oldest and rarest paintings were not painted on canvas, however, but on the walls of caves. To find such a treasure, you must brave the cave's current inhabitants: ferocious, hungry bears.

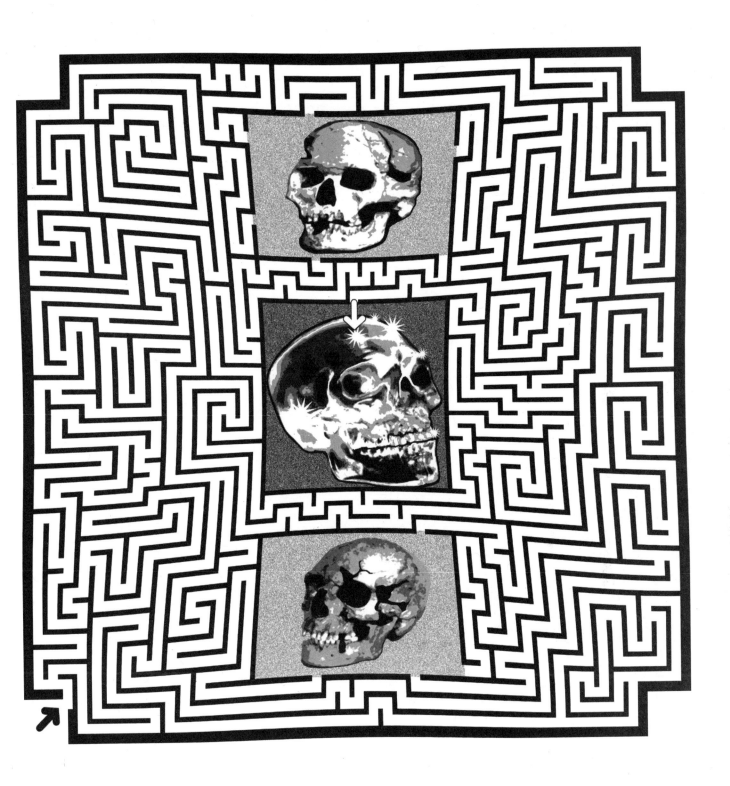

Ancient crystal skulls are highly valued—many people believe that these artifacts contain mystical properties. To reach the treasured crystal skull, however, you must search through the broken skulls of previous seekers.

An ornate golden mask is a fabulous treasure. Once used in ceremonies to impress and instill fear among the populace, it now watches over hordes of rats that are not easily intimidated. To reach this golden prize, therefore, you must avoid the swarms of vermin.

A precious statue made of gold and jewels waits to be claimed by the worthy. But, as if it were intended as a trap, it is surrounded by scorpions lying in wait. The careless and foolhardy will rush forward to grab the treasure, only to feel the scorpion's sting. Plan a careful course.

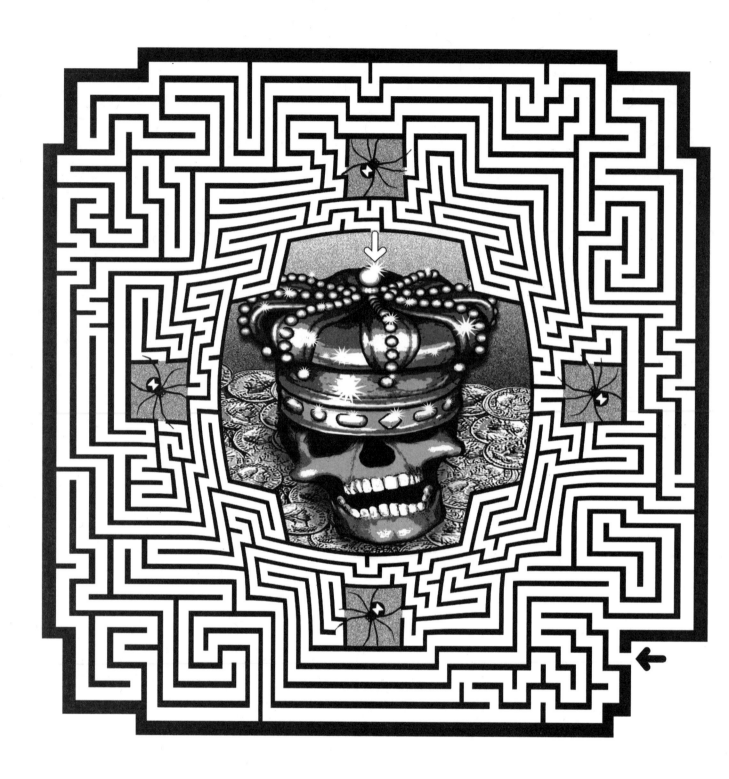

Kings and queens who once ruled civilizations all over the world are buried with vast amounts of wealth, enticing grave robbers to desecrate their resting places. Centuries of treasure seekers have found most of these treasures, yet some remain. Beware the black widows, or join the legions of lost souls.

The treasure of the Incas drove Spanish explorers mad with greed. Though much of the treasure was melted down and sent back to Spain, many believe that fabulous undiscovered bounty yet awaits discovery. To reach the treasure, however, you must brave cleverly positioned poisonous darts.

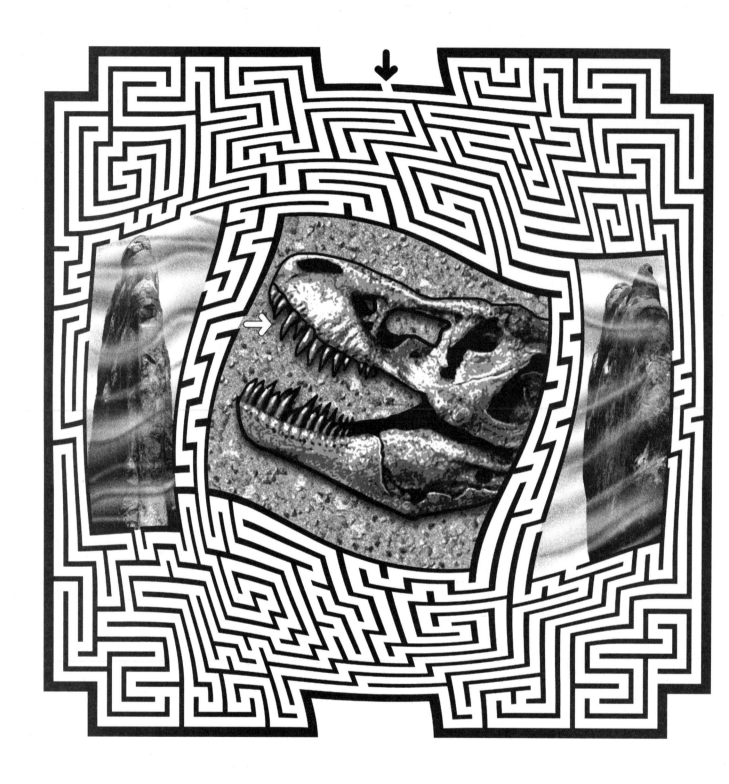

Treasures do not necessarily require the hand of man. The skull of a Tyrannosaurus Rex dinosaur, millions of years old, is a highly desirable find. Eons of weathering reveal fossilized remains. The windstorms that disclose such a treasure, however, can be very dangerous.

The greatest treasure yet discovered is the tomb of Tutankhamen (King Tut). It remained hidden for millennia until it was discovered in 1922 by Howard Carter and his team. Lord Carnarvon, who paid for the expedition, died of complications from a mosquito bite, starting the legend of a curse. Will you escape that fate?

Artifacts from crashed UFOs would be the greatest treasure ever discovered. Many believe such craft have already been retrieved but remain hidden from the public by cautious governments. If UFOs are real, then so are aliens—and they may not want their craft recovered!

Solutions

page 1

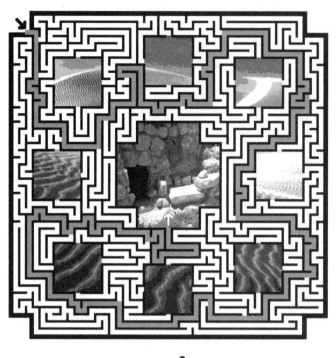

page 2

page 3

page 4

page 5

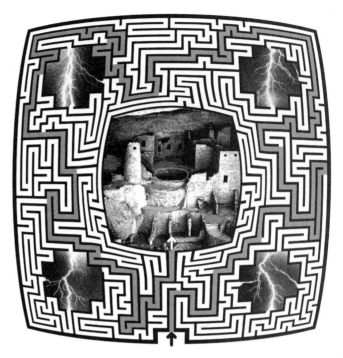

page 6

page 7

page 8

page 9

page 10

page 11

page 12

page 13

page 14

page 15

page 16

page 17

page 18

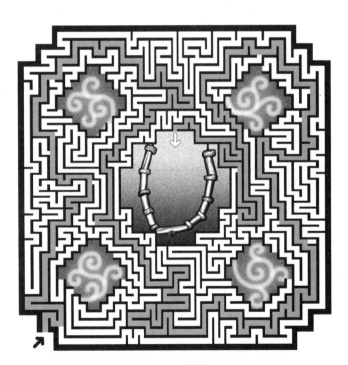

page 19

page 20

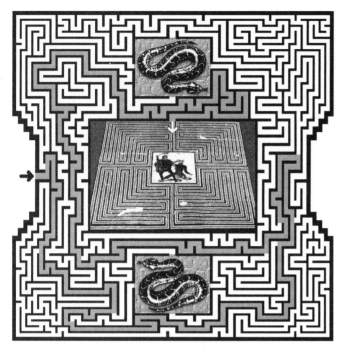

page 21

page 22

page 23

page 24

page 25

page 26

page 27

page 28

page 29

page 30

page 31

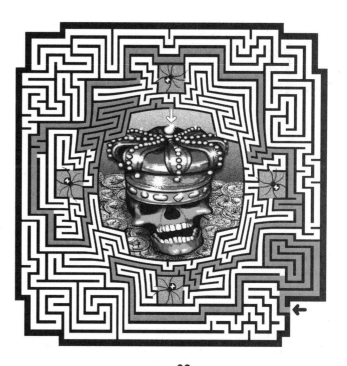

page 32

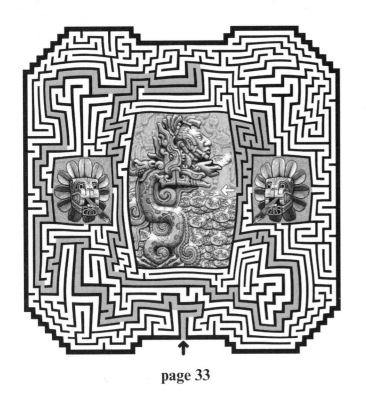

page 33

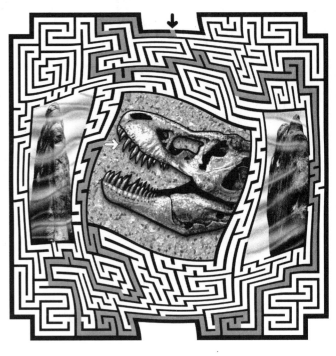

page 34

page 35

page 36